Loving God in Return
The Practice of Passionate Worship

Robert Schnase

ABINGDON PRESS
Nashville

Loving God in Return:
The Practice of Passionate Worship

Originally appeared in *Five Practices of Fruitful Living* by Robert Schnase,
which was published by Abingdon Press in 2010.

ISBN 978-1-6308-8300-3

14 15 16 17 18 19 20 21 22 23--10 9 8 7 6 5 4 3 2 1
MANUFACTURED IN THE UNITED STATES OF AMERICA

Contents

Loving God in Return
The Practice of Passionate Worship

*"You shall love the Lord your God with all **your** heart, and with all your soul, and with all your strength, and with all your mind; and your neighbor as yourself."*
—Luke 10:27

The Fruitful Living Series

Jesus taught a way of life and invited people into a relationship with God that was vibrant, dynamic and fruitful. He said, "I am the vine, you are the branches. Those who abide in me and I in them bear much fruit.... My father is glorified by this, that you bear much fruit and become my disciples," (John 15: 5, 8). Jesus wanted people to flourish.

Scripture is sprinkled with phrases that point to fruitful living—the kingdom of God, eternal life, immeasurable riches, a peace that passes all understanding, abundant life.

How do I cultivate a life that is abundant, fruitful, purposeful, and deep? What are the commitments, critical risks, and practices that open me to God's transforming grace and that help me discover the difference God intends for me to make in the world?

Loving God in Return

How do I live the fruitful, flourishing life of a follower of Christ?

Radical Hospitality. Passionate Worship. Intentional Faith Development. Risk-Taking Mission and Service. Extravagant Generosity.

Since the publication of *Five Practices of Fruitful Congregations,* these edgy, provocative, dangerous words have helped hundreds of congregations understand their mission, renew ministries, and stretch toward fruitfulness and excellence for the purposes of Christ.

The Fruitful Living Series moves the discussion of Christian practice from the congregational level to the personal practices of discipleship. The fruitful God-related life develops with intentional and repeated attention to five essential practices that are critical for our growth in Christ.

Radical Hospitality in our personal walk with Christ begins with an extraordinary receptivity to the grace of God. In distinctive and personal ways, we invite God into our hearts and make space for God in our lives. We receive God's love and offer it to others.

Through the practice of *Passionate Worship*, we learn to love God in return. We practice listening to God, allowing God to shape our hearts and minds through prayer, personal devotion, and community worship. We love God.

Through the practice of *Intentional Faith Development*, we do the soul work that connects us to others, immerses us in God's word, and positions us to grow in grace and mature in Christ. We learn in community.

The practice of *Risk-Taking Mission and Service* involves offering ourselves in purposeful service to others in need,

making a positive difference even at significant personal cost and inconvenience to our own lives. We serve.

Through the practice of *Extravagant Generosity*, we offer our material resources in a manner that supports the causes that transform life and relieve suffering and that enlarges the soul and sustains the spirit. We give back.

These five practices – to receive God's love, to love God in return, to grow in Christ, to serve others, and to give back—are so essential to growth in Christ and to the deepening of the spiritual life that failure to attend to them, develop them, and deepen them with intentionality limits our capacity to live fruitfully and fully, to settle ourselves completely in God, and to become instruments of God's transforming grace. The adjectives—*radical, passionate, intentional, risk-taking,* and *extravagant*—provoke us out of complacency and remind us that these practices require more than haphazard, infrequent, and mediocre attention.

These practices open our heart—to God, to others, to a life that matters, a life rich with meaning, relationship, and contribution. They help us flourish.

Christian Practice

The ministry of Jesus is grounded in personal practices. Jesus' life is marked by prayer, solitude, worship, reflection, the study of scripture, conversation, community, serving, engagement with suffering, and generosity. These personal practices sustained a ministry that opened people to God's grace, transformed human hearts, and changed the circumstances of people in need.

Christian practices are those essential activities we repeat and deepen over time. They create openings for God's spirit to shape us. Practices are not simply principles we talk about; practices are something we do. They make our faith a tangible and visible part of daily life. We see them done in the life of Jesus, and we do them until they become

a way of life for us. We become instruments of God's grace and love.

Through practice, we open ourselves to grace and let ourselves be opened by grace. We follow Christ, step by step, day by day, again and again; and by these steps and through these days, we are changed, we become someone different, we become new creations in Christ.

The books in this series are based on the premise that by repeating and deepening certain fundamental practices, we cooperate with God in our own growth in Christ and participate with the Holy Spirit in our own spiritual maturation. The fundamental practices are rooted in scripture and derived from the clear imperatives of the life of Christ. This isn't a self-improvement, pull-yourself-up-by-your-own-bootstraps notion of how we grow in grace. It's not about trying harder, working longer, or striving more to achieve God's blessing.

The Christian life is a gift of God, an expression of God's grace in Christ, the result of an undeserved and unmerited offering of love toward us. Every step of the journey toward Christ is preceded by, made possible by, and sustained by the perfecting grace of God.

The fruitful life is cultivated by placing ourselves in the most advantageous places to see, receive, learn, and understand the love that has been offered in Christ.

How to Use *The Fruitful Living Series*

The Fruitful Living Series is deeply personal, and as such it is composed of stories—the experiences, hopes, doubts, good efforts, and false starts of people like you and me. Faith journeys are used to illustrate key points so as to encourage honest reflection and conversation. But the approach is not individualistic—only about me, my, and mine. Every experience imbeds us more deeply in the community of Christ because it is in the presence of our sisters and brothers that our spirits are sustained, our hearts encouraged.

I pray for those who reach for these books searching for understanding about their own faith journeys, that it may stimulate them to deeper life in Christ. But I pray especially for those who have been handed these books and who open their pages reluctantly, that they may open themselves to the possibility that something in the stories and reflections

may cause them to think more deeply, pray more earnestly, and serve others in a more fruitful and satisfying way.

This series is experiential rather than systematic or dogmatic. It relies on the experiences of ordinary people who have been extraordinarily shaped by their relationship to God. None of us has the complete picture. Movement toward Christ is never a straight line, uninterrupted, obstacle free, totally consistent, predictable, and easily describable. There are no perfect accounts that capture everything that lies behind and no completely reliable maps that outline the future in one's faith journey. Soul work is hard, and following Christ is messy, challenging, joyous, scary, painful, sustaining, and frustratingly indescribable.

This *Fruitful Living Series* is about the everyday faith of everyday people seeking to listen for God, to love each other, to care for those in need, to embrace the stranger, to live the fruit of the spirit.

These books are practical. They are about what we do daily and intentionally, and about who we become because of how God uses what we do. They suggest a compass rather than map; a direction helpful for many diverse contexts rather than a specific step-by-step, how-to plan that fits only certain terrain.

Engage the material personally. Discover what you can learn about yourself, your relationship with God, your personal desires and internal resistances in the life of faith.

And read *The Fruitful Living Series* with others on the journey to Christ. Use it in house groups, adult Sunday school classes, a weeknight book study, or with your family. Resolve to deepen your own practices of faith. Pray for one another and support one another in Christ. Encourage church leaders and pastors to use the book in retreats, sermon series, or evening studies. These books focus the essential work that forms disciples; by cultivating these practices in the lives of those reached by the community

of faith, the congregation fulfills its mission of making disciples of Jesus Christ for the transformation of the world.

As a pastor and bishop, I've been granted the privilege of witnessing people whose faith is immeasurably greater than my own, whose sacrifice more than I myself could ever bear, whose impact in the lives of others through their service is immeasurably more than mine, whose personal discipline, depth of spirit, and maturing in Christ is far ahead of anything I shall ever achieve or hope to receive, and whose generosity is so extraordinary that it humbles me completely. This book is about how we learn from their fruitfulness in Christ so that we cooperate with God in becoming what God created us to be.

My prayer for you and your congregation is that *The Fruitful Living Series* helps us all grow in grace and in the knowledge and love of God. May we be changed from the inside out so that we can transform the world for the purposes of Christ.

1

RETURNING GOD'S LOVE CHANGES US

How lovely is your dwelling place,
O Lord of hosts!
My soul longs, indeed it faints
for the courts of the Lord;
my heart and my flesh sing for joy
to the living God.
—Psalm 84

Linda was in her early forties when her husband died, leaving her the task of raising two young children by herself. Neither her own family nor her husband's were church people, and she regarded Christianity with skepticism and Christians with suspicion. A few years after her husband's death, her daughters began attending youth activities at a church with their friends. Today, they were singing in the youth choir at the Sunday service, and Linda wanted to be present to support them.

With no church background, attending worship was daunting to her. When she walked in the door, several people offered greetings, shook her hand, and gave her leaflets. She wasn't sure where she was supposed to go and so she stood awkwardly watching the flow of people. As she entered the sanctuary, almost every pew already had people sitting at the ends, and she wasn't sure if she was supposed to step over them or ask them to move down to make room for her. She felt utterly self-conscious about every step she took. But she persevered and found a place near the back.

As the time for the service approached, music began and people quieted down. She sorted through the announcements about upcoming events. Some piqued her curiosity—a recovery workshop, a financial management class, a Habitat for Humanity project—and others remained a mystery to her, their purpose hidden behind acronyms she didn't understand, such as the Acts 28 Team, the Keystone Class, and an Alpha-Omega Circle meeting. A pastor began to speak, and the people around her responded in unison; then everyone stood and began to sing. Neither the tune nor the words were familiar to her, and she felt awkward following the music. For several minutes everything seemed a confusing mix of announcements, greetings, quotes from Scripture, and moving around. During the prayers, someone mentioned a family by name that had lost a loved one and requested prayers for them. There was silence as people throughout the sanctuary focused on the grieving family. Linda remembered how alone she felt when her husband had died, and she wondered how it must feel to be surrounded by people who are praying for you.

"What do the prayers do?" she wondered. She felt moved by the compassion of the gesture.

At last the youth choir moved forward, and she saw her daughters singing with their friends. A sense of parental satisfaction surged through her as she listened. The refrain was beautiful and catchy. She liked it. Later, the pastor told a story about a shepherd leaving the flock behind to search for the sheep that had gone astray. He said that the sheep had "nibbled its way lost," and Linda smiled at the line. That's how we get lost from God, the pastor said. We don't intend to, but we go from one tuft of grass to another until we end up somewhere we never imagined. And yet God loves us and searches for us and never gives up on any one of us. While Linda wasn't sure what she believed about God, the message made her think about her own life.

As the service ended, the mother of one of her daughter's friends came up to Linda and apologized for not noticing her sooner, gave her a gentle hug, and said how glad she

was to see her. "Next time you're here, let's sit together," the woman said. Something washed over Linda in that moment that was sudden and profound. The words touched her. She had never imagined returning for worship before that moment. As if a thread of grace had been cast across a great chasm, she felt a connection ever so tenuous and yet full of promise. She returned to her car and sat there for several minutes. "What do I do with this?" she asked herself. "What just happened?" The refrains of her daughter's voices were running through her mind, she was actually praying for a grieving family she didn't even know, she was thinking about that sheep nibbling its way lost, and she was smiling about the invitation to return.

A THREAD OF GRACE

"I always thought 'I'm praying for you' was a toss-away phrase, a polite way of expressing care when we don't know what else to say . . . then my father had a heart attack," Stephanie says. "A coworker said she would pray for me. She pulled out a notebook and wrote down my father's name. Later in the evening she called me to ask how I was doing. In the midst of the fear and uncertainty, I didn't feel alone anymore. Someone genuinely cared."

Prayer casts threads of grace across chasms of disconnection, loneliness, fear, and pain. Prayer weaves people back into community and rebinds them to the source of life.

Our Love for God

Worship expresses our love for God, our devotion to the creator, redeemer, and sustainer of life. Our response to God's great love for us is to love others and to serve them, and also to express our adoration to God. We love God in return. We open ourselves to God's Spirit so we can see the world through God's eyes. Worship involves voluntarily setting time aside to focus on God's will rather than our own agenda, to receive God's word rather than merely giving our point of view. We offer ourselves anew to God's purposes rather than trying to fit God neatly into our own goals. A sustained pattern and practice of worship lends coherence, meaning, depth, and connection to our lives. Worship reconfigures our interior lives and aligns us with the life of Christ. Worship connects us to God.

Worship changes us. Understanding the meaning of worship requires looking beyond *what people do* to see with the eyes of faith *what God does*. God uses worship to

crack open closed hearts, reconcile broken relationships, renew hope, restrain harmful arrogance, heal wounded souls, shape personal decisions, interrupt destructive habits, stimulate spiritual growth, and transform lives. God reshapes the human soul through worship.

Since ancient times, people have gathered to seek God through prayer, story, music, song, fellowship, and mutual compassion. *Synagogue* means "to bring together." God lives in the people gathered in devotion and covenant. And the Latin word *ecclesia*, the root of our word for church, means "called out of the world." God calls us out of the ordinary life of work, family, and leisure into the presence of the sacred so that we can develop the spiritual resources that guide and sustain fruitful living.

Worship is the reason God liberated the Hebrew people from the oppressions of slavery. God spoke to Moses, saying, "Release my people so they can worship me" (Exodus 8:1, *The Message*). God desires our devotion.

Jesus presents the highest of God's desires this way, "That you love the Lord your God with all your passion and prayer and muscle and intelligence—and that you love your neighbor as well as you do yourself" (Luke 10:27, *The Message*). Heart, mind, soul, and strength—in worship we offer all to God in love.

Worship provides the most likely setting for the change of heart and mind we describe as *justification*, the moment of conscious awareness and decision that involves our receiving God's grace through Christ, confessing our need for God, accepting God's pardon, and turning our lives toward God and away from former ways. Jesus tells the story of the Pharisee and the tax collector entering the temple (Luke 18:9-14). The Pharisee is so full of himself that he is unable to open himself to God. The tax collector, consciously aware of his brokenness and spiritual emptiness, genuinely offers his heart to God. Jesus says the tax collector leaves a different person than when he came in. He is *justified*—by grace his life freshly aligns with God.

He discovers a new relationship with God through open-hearted worship and devotion to God.

In the Gospels, Jesus and his followers regularly attend temple, read from Scripture, speak of giving, practice prayer, retreat to God, give thanks, and observe the sabbath. Worship becomes their natural breath. Worship strengthens them for ministry. Living in God involves returning God's love.

REFLECTION

That you LOVE *the Lord your God with all your* PASSION *and* PRAYER *and* MUSCLE *and* INTELLIGENCE—*and that you* LOVE *your* NEIGHBOR *as well as you do* YOURSELF

—*Luke 10:27*, The Message

Our response to God's great love for us is to love others and to serve them, and also to express our adoration to God. We love God in return.

Questions

- What are your earliest memories of worship? What made the greatest impression on you?

- Do you enjoy worship? What causes you delight?

- What sustains you in worship? What impacts you the most and what influences you the least?

- When was a time you felt connected to God in worship?

- When has a worship experience changed your heart and mind and provided you with fresh spiritual insights?

Prayer

Lord, cause me to be what you have called me to be: shaped by your Spirit and changed by my love for Christ. Make me right with you; align me with your love.

WHY DO WE WORSHIP?

> *Make a joyful noise to the LORD,*
> *all the earth.*
> *Worship the LORD with gladness;*
> *come into his presence with singing.*
> *—Psalm 100:1-2*

What happens in worship, and why is it important? First, worship is the way we orient ourselves toward God. If God's unconditional love is the pivotal truth of life, how do we set aside time to focus on God, to receive God's love, and to love God in return? Worship connects us to God and to other people who also self-consciously choose to orient themselves toward God. God desires a relationship with us, and in response to God's seeking us, worship is our way of seeking God, our reaching upward to God's reaching downward.

Second, worship fosters our relationship to the transcendent, spiritual aspects of life. We temporarily push other more tangible and mundane things aside to discover more mysterious and sacred elements and to approach them with awe and openness. We put spiritual and relational things first.

Many of life's most critical questions cannot be answered through more information, with better science, or by

linear modes of intellectual exploration. Questions of meaning, purpose, love, suffering, connection, life, death, and hope require a more elastic and searching form of knowledge. Spiritual insight, while as true and eternal as the laws of gravity, requires grasping certainties that are not describable principally by fact or science, but by experience, trust, and grace. When we gather to deal with facets of life for which there are no easy or explicit answers, we find ourselves exploring the wonderfully transcendent parts of our existence. In the beyondness of silence, prayer, reflection, music, embrace, ritual, and community, we discover insight, sustenance, beauty, and awe. Like a breeze—felt but never seen—the Spirit feeds our wild need for wonder, our essential search for meaning.

Human beings are not oriented merely by one sense or two, but by many. Imagine a room full of people; one third understand and speak only German, another third only Spanish, and another third only English. If we speak only one language, we leave two-thirds of the people

unaddressed, and we cannot receive the gift of their insight and knowledge. If we want to communicate with all of them and receive the resources they offer us, we will have to learn to communicate in other languages.

Likewise with the interior life: perhaps only one third of the knowledge and wisdom to live meaningfully is reducible to and reachable by conscious, linear, rational thought. This we learn through words, sermons, and the sharing of ideas. But another third of insight and experience that expands our sense of meaning, motivation, and connection comes to us through music, silence, movement, liturgy, and a host of other means. These are truths we absorb in ways beyond our conscious awareness. Nevertheless, they form us, strengthen us, and connect us to God and one another. For instance, it is a mystery that breaking bread and sharing wine makes us one and forms us into the body of Christ, but it does. Communion is an outward sign of an inward grace, a visible reminder of a mysteriously spiritual truth.

Receiving bread and wine, viewing artistry in stained glass, kneeling alongside others, bowing our heads, singing songs that lift the soul, meditating upon the cross, offering our gifts—these feed us and form us with truths beyond verbal articulation. And another third of insight and truth comes through the experience of being together with others, our sense of belonging. By praying for one another, serving and receiving Communion, and harmonizing our voices in song, we discover the grace of community. Navigating the unknown and uncertain seas of life—of suffering and healing, of disconnection and reconciliation, of life and death—we realize through worship that we are all on the same ship sailing toward the same port. Worship grants us a coherent sense of belonging, of purpose, and of future.

Practicing worship is like learning other languages that open us to the full resources of the spiritual life. God's transcendent love pulls us out of ourselves, stretches us, and takes us beyond where we could possibly arrive on our

own. Realities beyond conscious reach become accessible to us. God is present in silence, ritual, music, and movement as we grasp the powerlessness of our words to describe the meaning and grace of community.

God's presence fills the room, embracing us, creating a sense of belonging discernable to those who receive it, known to us without our seeing it, present before we consciously ask for it or realize it. Through worship we rise up and soar.

The Most Advantageous Place

Third, worship is our way of putting ourselves in the most advantageous place for engaging the Spirit. While God is present in all of life, it is through worship that we purposefully search for God and become acutely aware of God's presence. We give our attention to God, and focus on God's revelation rather than merely our own. We listen

for God with greater intentionality. God may be present anywhere—including at the golf course or on our back patio or in the great outdoors. However, our reason for being in those other places is not explicitly to search for God, to notice God, listen for God, or open our souls to God's heart and God's people.

Worship represents a regular appointment with the sacred, a planned encounter, a scheduled time and place to connect. We arrive with souls prepared, minds ready, and hearts open; and our anticipation makes worship different from other times. Our singing and praying together represent a conscious choice to form a rhythm of engagement with the spiritual elements of life that balances our engagement with the world. We could spend our Sundays in a thousand different ways, many of them positive and helpful. We could choose to work, but instead of being materially productive today we choose to focus on God. We could choose to play, sleep, or exercise; but instead we've decided that our relationship with God is of

such importance that we've set those things aside to attend to this pivotal relationship.

Fourth, worship brings us back to ourselves. People frequently describe worship as the activity during their week that centers them, grounds them, connects them, or anchors them. All these words reveal the risk we feel of losing touch, becoming distracted, unfocused, and disconnected, or living haphazard and harried lives rather than feeling rooted and grounded in what really matters. In worship we "sing our shadows home," as an ancient Native American story tells. We come back to ourselves.

Worship carves out a time to focus on the larger questions of life, of end and purpose. It lifts our eyes beyond the immediate and tangible to look at life from a wider perspective. We have time to reflect, anticipate, reprioritize, and to push the reset button in our spiritual lives when we might otherwise veer off course from our most vital relationships. A tragic undercurrent of our culture is

IMPRESSIONS OF GRACE

"When I visited her at her nursing home, she no longer recognized me. She did not even know where she lived, and she seemed quite agitated. It was disheartening," Ann says of her grandmother with Alzheimer's. "But when someone began to play 'Amazing Grace' on the piano, my grandmother's face glowed, she sang the words from memory, tears fell from her eyes, and she settled into her seat with a sense of calm. I was astonished, and grateful."

Worship runs deep. Music, prayers, and liturgy leave lifelong impressions that lend coherence, support, and connection beyond what we can comprehend.

how many people feel lost within their families, within their communities, within their world. Worship provides purpose, correction, and a sense of community. Worship helps us catch our breath, prepare, reunite, and renew. Worship provides a way by which we let ourselves be found, a way to find God, and to find ourselves.

Through prayers, music, sermon, and sacrament, we remember (literally, *re-member*), enfolding ourselves once more into the body of people who follow Jesus. Worship reminds us that we belong to God and to one another, and this sense of belonging is essential for our spiritual well-being. The repeated metaphors of unity—one body, one bread, one baptism, one God, one family in which we all are sisters and brothers in Christ—weave us into a community of mutual care and compassion that sustains us. We bind ourselves to one another and to God during worship so that during the challenging times throughout the week, we do not become unbound. In worship, we love because we are loved.

From God's Point of View

The purpose of worship does not begin and end with what human beings do; worship is the means God uses to accomplish God's purposes in the human heart and in the community of Christ. God is active in worship even when we are not. God speaks to us. God accomplishes the continuing reconciliation of the world through worship.

Imagine worship from God's point of view. What does God seek through our gathering to love and serve God? Does God need our praise? God desires our praise because by praising God we open our hearts to God's love and direct our hearts toward the following of God's ways. God's desire for our praise reveals God's desire for what is best for us. In worship, God offers a setting for us to confess our brokenness, receive pardon, and relieve our guilt. God works with us to reconstruct a pathway that leads to greater

fullness. God plants seeds in our heart and soul with the anticipation that some of these will take root and grow within us. In worship, God, the gardener of the soul, clears the weeds, waters the seeds of hope and courage, helps us blossom in love and flourish into wonderfully fruitful lives. Worship itself, and every element of it, is a means of grace, a way for God to accomplish our re-creation.

People enter worship with eagerness, yearning, and devotion. They offer themselves passionately, and they anticipate God's presence. "My soul longs, indeed it faints, / for the courts of the LORD" (Psalm 84:2). They seek God. Passionate Worship describes the practice of those for whom worship is not merely routine or performance, but a means of connecting to God. Passionate Worship feeds a dynamic, vibrant, fruitful relationship with God.

Passion means full of life, involving our whole selves—mind, body, and spirit. People who love God passionately

enter worship with eagerness, anticipation, expectation, a yearning for God. They are drawn by their love for God rather than by feeling expected to attend a social function. Passionate Worship has as its source and purpose the desire to connect ourselves to God and to God's people. Passionate Worship is authentic rather than contrived, from the heart rather than merely going through motions. *Passion* means inflamed with love and refers to our desire to open ourselves entirely to God, inviting God's Spirit to permeate us completely. Through Passionate Worship, we love God in return, and through our continuing practice we stay in love with God.

Worship settles us in God, and anchors us in Christ. *Passion* connotes doing something with such fullness of feeling that our love pushes us through all the hesitations and doubts and setbacks that might otherwise give us pause. Passionate Worship expresses our desire to put God at the center of our lives.

In theology, *the Passion* refers to the complete outpouring of Jesus Christ, the offering of himself, even to death on a cross, in order to complete our relationship with God through Christ. In the Passion of Christ, we receive grace upon grace. The sacrifice of Christ—Jesus' life, death, and resurrection—is the turning point of our relationship with God and the center-point of our worship. In the Passion of Christ, God reaches for us. In our passionate response, we reach for God.

The path to fruitful living, to discovering the riches of the spiritual life, involves practicing worship seriously and with committed consistency, rather than attending worship haphazardly, infrequently, and without enough consistency to feel at home and confident about worshipping God. Truly cultivating a relationship with God requires a conscious effort to make the practice of worship a lifelong priority.

WITHOUT A SOUND

Imagine that you were unable to hear the sounds of worship in your congregation and you could only observe with your eyes. What would you see in the faces of people as they arrived? Would you see warmth, receptivity, eagerness? Boredom, anxiety, impatience? Would people appear self-absorbed or focused on others? Would they appear happy to be present or anxious to leave? What would their body language and posture and responses to others reveal? What would people see in your eyes and by your behavior? Would they see grace?

REFLECTION

Jesus said to them,
"COME AWAY
to a deserted place
ALL BY YOURSELVES
and **REST** *a while."*

—*Mark 6:31*

> *Worship provides a way*
> *by which we let ourselves be found,*
> *a way to find God,*
> *and a way to find ourselves.*

Questions

- What replenishes your spirit and refreshes you in worship? How does God use worship to speak to you?

- How has worship changed you over time?

- How has participating in worship shaped the relationships you have with your family? With your community?

- How does worship help you see the world through God's eyes? And what difference does this make for you?

Prayer

Open the eyes of my heart, Lord, so that I may see your extraordinary presence among us in our ordinary worship each week. Help me remember you, and discover you, in each prayer and song and sermon and sacrament.

The Practice of Passionate Worship

THE MYSTERY OF WORSHIP

The Master, Jesus, on the night of his betrayal, took bread. Having given thanks, he broke it and said, This is my body, broken for you.
Do this to remember me.
— I Corinthians 11:23-24 The Message

Any attempt to completely describe worship falls short. In ways we cannot fully comprehend, we practice visible and tangible behaviors which result in our feeling sustained, grounded, forgiven, connected, motivated to make better choices, and called to serve others. How that happens often remains beyond conscious awareness or description. Worship is mystery.

Why does repeating the history of God's grace, praying, giving God thanks, kneeling with others, and receiving a piece of bread and a taste of grape juice affect us? I have received the sacrament of Holy Communion and presided over its liturgy thousands of times, and yet I feel utterly inadequate explaining why and how participating in this simple ritual affects the human spirit. That the breaking of bread makes us one and that the receiving of it makes us whole are true, but how this works is beyond my capacity to comprehend or explain. It is mystery.

At times I'm overwhelmed by the immediate sense of the sacrament's power; it consciously and presently affects me. As I'm repeating the words, receiving bread, or watching other people do so, I discern a palpable sense of being deeply affected. An elderly couple support each other in their kneeling and rising; a family with young children huddle together to take the bread; varied languages and accents carry the whispered responses; people step forward carrying unbearable grief, secret joy, unspoken remorse, and newfound resolve. Watch those who step forward one after another, and meditate on all that their lives represent. What do all these people have in common? All of them remember God's love in Christ, taking Christ's broken body into themselves, and temporarily orient themselves once more toward the ultimate revelation of God's love for each of us. They take Christ's life as their own. Worship blesses us.

People stepping forward to receive the sacrament become a fine tapestry interwoven by the Holy Spirit into one people. They are one with each other, one with Christ, and one in ministry to the world. In this simple act, they become community; communion with Christ becomes real, and they experience a sense of belonging not merely to the people present in the room but to all those who have gone before and who will follow. They form and reinforce an identity and spiritual bond with all who voluntarily receive into themselves the sacrificial love of God in Christ. Once more they become new persons in Christ.

Every single hour since the middle of the first century, somewhere in our world people have taken bread and broken it, calling it the body of Christ, and have given it to one another to remember Christ. They have used roughly the same words and told the same story in hundreds of languages. When we break the bread, we join a company of people that extends around the entire world as well as back in history, forward into the future, and upward to

eternity. Even if we repeat it a million times, we never fully comprehend its meaning and impact. It is mystery.

There are times I can sense the unifying presence of the Holy Spirit in the sacrament as surely as I feel the bread in my fingers. Other times I feel like I'm repeating a perfunctory ritual and reading words by rote. People with tears streaming down their faces at the spiritual power of the moment kneel alongside others who roll their eyes at the seeming nonsense of it all. How can this be? The bread itself does not change its substance, and afterward remains merely bread as beforehand. But through our remembering Christ and his conscious commitment to the salvation of the world and by inviting the Spirit's presence, we change the use of these ordinary elements. As their purpose changes, we are changed. Through the eyes of faith, these are no longer merely ordinary bread and wine but the body and blood of Christ. We're taking Christ into us as God is taking us into the body of Christ. Is the change in our lives perceptible? Sometimes yes. Sometimes no. Yet, by repeating the sacrament, the practice has a mysteriously

formative impact on our lives. The ritual becomes a means of grace, a revealing in tangible form of an intangible and invisible truth.

Truth, love, and creativity always come from places we never fully comprehend. By feeding the mind, heart, and soul by these motions and words, we give the Spirit space to play, to move around the deep places inside us and shake us up, to take root and to expand within us. Thoughts that weren't there in us before are now there. Beyond conscious awareness, something below the surface goes on, something real and life-changing. The regular repeating of the sacrament creates us anew.

Likewise with other sacraments and services, their effect and meaning are both mysterious and real. God loves us even before we represent God's grace with the sacrament of baptism; we give our hearts to Christ even before the confirming words we speak aloud; we belong to the body

A CONVERTING SACRAMENT

While receiving the broken bread in his hands, Carl felt struck by the reconciling sacrifice of Christ. He thought about his brother with whom he had not spoken for more than five years, and the brokenness he sensed. In an unexpected moment of clarity, he realized how much responsibility he himself carried for the disconnection. "Life is too short, and someone has to take the first step," he thought. That afternoon, he phoned his brother and began a conversation. An uneasy and awkward beginning blossomed into a more comfortable pattern of phone calls over the months that followed. By reconnecting to his brother, Carl filled a part of himself that was empty.

Communion is not merely a confirming sacrament that reassures us of our belonging to the community of Christ; it is a converting sacrament God uses to reframe our hearts and redirect our behaviors.

of Christ even without the membership pledge that makes our intentions known; a couple's love for each other is real prior to the wedding vows that make their covenant public; God receives our spirits whether we utter words of faith at the funeral or not. But in our saying and doing these things, deep invisible hopes and graces become tangible, visible, and public. Our highest yearnings and God's deepest desires rise up to expressible and accessible levels. Mysteriously, our rituals make all the more true what is already the case! They connect us to God.

Music Lifts Us to God

Music is another aspect of worship that connects us with God. It is a mystery how music shapes the human spirit, but it does. Music makes us happy—to sing it, hear it, and share it. And music moves us to profound contemplation, reaching depths that are otherwise inaccessible by mere words or intentional reflection. Music helps us say things

we have trouble speaking in words. It offers a means to proclaim our love for God that comes not only from the conventional thoughts of our minds, but from the more emotive, heartfelt, spontaneous parts in our souls. With music, we discover accents of wonder and dimensions of awe that are otherwise inexpressible. Music lifts us to God.

Music remains with us, embedding rhythms, tunes, and words within us without our even knowing it. Music is a principal means by which we explore, discover, and receive spirituality. Music opens the door to the interior life and helps us bring God into daily life.

The melodies of European hymn writers, the rhythms of the people of Africa, the cadence of Native American influences, the acoustic American folk sounds—all branches of the Christian family have used music to reach for God, to listen to God, and to praise God. Slaves in America used music to bind their hearts to God and one another, to inspire courage, to relieve suffering, and to express their aspirations for freedom. Slaves found the passageway to

another reality through music, preaching, and worship. Music provided not an escape from but an embracing of reality that granted a measure of spiritual freedom that paved the way to political freedom. Christians sing their way to new life.

Music, in its practical aspects, affects us by writing truths upon our hearts in a manner that we carry with us wherever we go. We learn the content of the faith more easily with the rhyme and rhythm of lyrics and music. How many times we find the refrains from recent worship replaying through our minds—*Amazing grace how sweet the sound . . . Our God is an awesome God . . . Because he lives I can face tomorrow . . .* Music makes spiritual truths poetic and memorable. Music grants the pleasure and leisure to ruminate unconsciously upon meanings long after we consciously repeat them. When we leave worship, music goes with us and carries us forward into the week.

Music has an undeniable unifying effect. Where else do nonmusicians join their voices with others to sing? Rarely outside of national anthems and carols at Christmas parties do people experience singing together with others. We are unpracticed in the power of singing together and what that means.

Singing together rehearses community. Sharing our individual gifts leads to community outcomes that far exceed the sum of the individual parts. Harmonizing voices reflects the harmony with others we seek in the world. Singing lifts us out of ourselves and binds us together.

Music touches places in our soul where no sermon could ever reach, penetrating where no words could ever go. Music puts spirit into us, raises us up, and takes us soberly to face our own mortality. Sermons inform us in important ways, but music takes us on a trip to the other side of our brains where fact, data, rationality, and objectivity

end like a pier extending over a sea with unfathomable depths. Music allows us to jump into the deeper waters of the soul and into aspects of community and grace that we cannot begin to consciously understand. Music caresses the unconscious and subconscious and preconscious parts of the human psyche. Why would we not be curious to discover and recover its power? Music helps us attend to something both primitive and present, both elemental and sophisticated. It's hard to imagine the spiritual life without music and the world it opens to us. And yet how it affects us remains a mystery. Music is a means of grace.

Affectionate Attention

Perhaps the greatest mystery involves how the affectionate attention to ordinary things in worship—prayer, music, liturgy, Scripture, sacrament, word, offering, fellowship—reveals a beauty, depth, meaning, and coherence that opens us to the discovery and rediscovery of grace in

everyday situations throughout the week. Worship trains our attentiveness to God, attunes us to noticing the Spirit. Not only does it help us perceive things anew during the worship service itself, it helps us see things in everyday life we never saw before. Our quality of attention to God improves; and we begin to see God's work, sense God's presence, and discern God's call more naturally. In worship, we give our hearts to God. One hour each week changes all the other hours of our week.

Worship is mystery, and part of our task is not merely to wrestle with the mystery or seek to avoid it, but to embrace it and receive it.

Personal Devotion

Another way we express our love to God through worship is in our daily prayers and devotions. People who practice loving God in return carve out time in each day to

intentionally focus on God, express gratitude, offer private confession, and lift petitions and intercessions. Prayer at fixed times, such as morning prayers when rising, grace before meals, or evening prayers at the close of the day, helps us create a space in our lives for God. Daily habit provides the same restorative, centering, and encouraging quality to daily life that community worship adds to weekly life. Short devotional reading, reciting a prayer, or the simple observance of silence settles us in God. We orient ourselves a little each day toward God. Daily prayer blesses us.

We can't develop a meaningful relationship with someone if we don't spend time with them. The same is true with our relationship with God. Daily prayer and private worship is time with God.

Frequently, we cling too tightly to anger, blame, hate, hurt, grief, guilt, and sadness. How can we restore our

souls, heal our brokenness, and relieve our fear? Daily prayer filters our experiences through our relationship with God. Through patterns of personal devotion, we perceive life differently, regulate negative emotions, and lift them up to God. Through prayer, we see even the most intransigent and painful experiences as pathways to new life. Prayer helps us face the darkness inside while reaching for the light. One kind of experience becomes something else entirely through prayer as we move toward transformation, resurrection, and a continuing rebirth. Prayer gives us courage to choose paths that lead to life.

Personal prayer changes our relationships with friends, coworkers, strangers, and even those toward whom we feel animosity. The places in ourselves that are most disconnected from God, when explored persistently and honestly in prayer, lead us also to reconciliation with others. We repair disconnection with others through soul work; inner peace reaps an outward harvest.

Daily personal devotion prepares us for community worship. God's ability to reach us increases as we cooperate with the Holy Spirit in making ready our souls to receive God's Word. Personal prayer fosters eagerness for community worship.

Resistances

Someone new to following Jesus or with little experience may find starting or returning to a regular pattern of worship a daunting task. Stepping into a gathering of people who sing, pray, stand, sit, or kneel for reasons we don't understand makes us feel awkward. And yet this is true for any new experience—learning tennis, joining a fitness club, beginning a new friendship. We feel a little foolish, clumsy, and self-conscious before we develop a comfortable confidence that makes continuing on feel worthwhile. A nourishing pattern of worship takes time and commitment.

Any commitment exists in a context of competing obligations, habits, and interests. To move in one direction means forgoing other directions. To attend worship with frequency and consistency means reprioritizing time and making the effort. Worship results from intentionality.

Sometimes attending worship requires acting against the resistance, criticism, or ridicule of a spouse or friend. Seeking God is overtly countercultural in many contexts. Following Christ requires the capacity to handle the stress of going our own way and making our own decisions without the support of others we love. If you feel called to return to worship, do so. Do not wait for the day when everyone agrees to come with you. Your friends love the *old* you; they will love the *new* you as well, but it takes time for that to emerge, and we cannot let friends undermine our efforts to explore the spiritual life. Worship requires resolve.

Sometimes attending worship feels difficult because we are not sure we really believe all that following Jesus seems to involve. And yet beliefs emerge and rise to greater clarity through the practice of worship and by belonging to a community of faith. No one takes the first steps toward Christ by comprehending all the nuances of faith at once. At times, people worship, not to express something with absolute certainty, but in order not to remain altogether silent about what they intuitively feel: that they yearn for peace; that they desire to align themselves with what is good and just; and that they desire to serve others, explore spirituality, and learn to love. These motivate us even when we cannot express our underlying beliefs with clarity or in theological terms. Worship suggests trust.

Everyone also faces internal resistances, and most people backslide occasionally in their personal or public commitments to worship. Our faith life fluctuates between times of curiosity and tedium, exhilaration and ordinariness, doubt and rediscovery. By stepping back in and repeating

familiar prayers both when they make perfect sense and when they puzzle us completely, worship anchors us. Making the effort to stay connected is difficult but important. When we start a fresh pattern of worship, everything in our life pulls against the new practice to restore the old habits that existed previously. The courage to start leads to the strength to continue. Worship takes persistence.

We worship because we love God. We do it to connect to other people. We do it to find ourselves. We discover a whole new world. Worship fosters joy, connection, self-understanding, and meaning. God desires to connect with us and to connect us to others. Worship lifts us, humbles us, motivates us, and pulls us out of ourselves. Worship fundamentally changes us.

As for all the practices, a pattern of passionate worship requires a surrendering, a yielding of ourselves and of our will, a giving up of some good things in order to attend

to greater things. Surrender involves trust, openness, and vulnerability. Following Christ involves an incremental relinquishing of our control in order to allow God's Spirit to form us anew. To "have in us the mind that is in Christ" is a gradual process, a maturing, a becoming. There are no experts, only learners, and those who have stepped down the path a little farther than we have. We gradually feel less awkward, more connected, more confident in the face of the resistances, and immeasurably more aware of the blessings that accrue with falling in love with God. Worship God.

REFLECTION

This is **MY BODY, BROKEN** *for* **YOU.** *Do this to* **REMEMBER ME.**

—*I Corinthians 11:24*, The Message

Our highest yearnings and God's deepest desires rise up to expressible and accessible levels. Mysteriously, our rituals make all the more true what is already the case! They connect us to God.

Questions

- What aspect of worship creates for you the greatest sense of cohesion and connection to others? What aspect expresses mystery?
- Think of an experience of Holy Communion that particularly moved you. What made it especially meaningful? How does Holy Communion shape your connection to God and God's people?
- Have you felt your spirit moved or lifted up to God by music in worship? How does singing make a difference in your spiritual life?
- How do your daily prayers help you connect to God? How has praying with others helped you feel God's Spirit at work?
- When was a time you felt discomfort or resistance to the experience of worship? How do you work through this?

Prayer

Help me remember, dear God, that in returning to you, I find strength; in resting in you, I find peace; and in trusting you, I find quietness.

RENEWING OUR LOVE FOR GOD

But what happens when we live God's way? He brings gifts into our lives, much the same way that fruit appears in an orchard—things like affection for others, exuberance about life, serenity.
—*Galatians 5:22-23a*, The Message

People who practice Passionate Worship attend worship frequently and consistently until it becomes a valued and sustaining pattern for them. Worship becomes a priority and they shift schedules to attend when conflicts arise. They love worship because they love God.

They honor God by availing themselves of the sacraments, becoming familiar with the constituent parts of the worship service, receiving the musical offerings of the choir or band, and opening their minds to the Scriptures and sermon. They open themselves to God's Word as a means of loving.

They enter worship with hearts and minds prepared. They eagerly anticipate how God may connect to them. They read the Scriptures in advance. They pray for the pastor, the church staff, the musicians, and all who lead worship. They take notes when something strikes them so they can mull it over in private. They ask themselves, "What is God saying to me today through the songs, the

Scripture and sermon, the sacrament, or the fellowship of others?" Loving God means listening for God.

People who practice Passionate Worship let music into their souls. They lift their voices in praise to God. They let themselves sing.

People who love worship offer their services to enhance the experience for others. If they are able, they sing in the choir or praise band, serve as ushers, greeters, lay readers, or Communion servers, or they help prepare the worship space. They create a sense of warmth and welcome for others. They influence an atmosphere of expectation. Worship is the most important hour of the week.

They carry their daily lives with them into prayer and worship, and carry worship and prayer with them into their daily lives. They live so that their whole life glorifies and praises God.

They are people of prayer. They pray in a style that sustains them. Some find a quiet time each morning and others do so at night; some take walks to orient themselves toward God and others meet with friends; some use printed prayers and devotions and others open themselves spontaneously; some kneel, others sit, and still others pray during exercise; some pray at home and others at the office. They make time to pray.

They read about prayer, learn about prayer, pray with others and develop the habit of prayer. They practice prayer until it feels as natural as breathing. They teach their children to pray. They may keep a prayer list of people and concerns. Prayer for them becomes more than asking things of God. They listen for God and discern what God asks of them. They cultivate the gifts of silence and waiting. Clarity is born in spiritual stillness. They create times to pause, rest, listen, and prepare themselves for God. They pray without ceasing.

They love God, and they invest themselves wholeheartedly in cultivating their relationship with God. They let God reach them and change them through worship. They foster the spiritual life.

Helen

Helen grew up active in the Christian faith. At her baptism as an infant, her parents vowed to support her growth in grace. As a young girl, Helen loved worship. She learned songs in vacation Bible school, led youth services, and worshiped outdoors at summer camp. At confirmation, she committed herself to follow Christ. At her wedding, she and her husband made public their covenant before God. Helen adapted patterns of worship with each phase of her life, shaped by the activities of her children and her own changing needs. Frequently, Helen assisted with Communion, served as a lay reader of Scripture, worked as an usher, or volunteered for the worship committee.

She became one of those people to whom others instinctively turn for insight and counsel. She wore the mantle of spiritual encourager with great humility. She was even-tempered, warm, open, and gracious.

Helen loved Scripture, and each year would sign up to participate in Bible study. Helen's comments had a different quality to them, profoundly personal, reflective, and engaging. Scripture was not merely about people "over there, back then," but about our own lives. She'd quietly say, "I feel that God may be telling me something through this story . . ." She allowed herself to be shaped by God's Spirit.

For instance, a single sermon stimulated her to organize a prayer group. She and five of her friends met weekly for years to encourage one another's growth in Christ. In another sermon, she sensed God's call to initiate a literacy tutoring ministry among immigrant families. A service

about tithing set her on the path of increased giving, and this inspired her to teach others the spiritual significance of generosity. Through a *Walk to Emmaus* retreat, she felt the Spirit prompt her to a deeper life of prayer and of teaching prayer. The retreat invigorated her love for Holy Communion, and she came to regard the sacrament as one of the most important practices of her spiritual life.

Helen's rich interior life overflowed into the lives of other people. At times she'd step into the church office and ask if she could pray with me. In stressful situations, she'd remind me, "Perhaps there's something God thinks you need to learn from this." Prayer, she'd remind me, was about desiring God, not just desiring something from God. Her soul work helped others with theirs.

She invited people into the life of the church, intuitively knowing the right things to say and do to make guests

feel at home in worship. She made room in the church for strangers, becoming a friend and encourager.

Helen was diagnosed with cancer when she was in her midfifties. For two years she faced the uncertain and anguishing rhythm of progress and setback. All those people she had loved came back into her own life as caregivers and prayer partners. She grew weaker physically, but continued to strengthen everyone around. Friends and family gathered with her for a service of healing. They shared Communion and surrounded her with prayer. People found themselves overwhelmed by her graciousness, her sense of peace, and the ease by which she accepted death itself as a kind of grace. Her funeral was a celebration of life, an expression of gratitude to God for a life well-lived. Helen taught us how to live, and how to die.

Helen was deep-hearted, generous, grounded, and wise. She became that kind of person through a lifetime of worship.

Imagine if we could extract from Helen's life all the formative worship experiences that impacted her. Imagine if we could remove from her heart, mind, and soul all the thousands of worship services; tens of thousands of hymns, sermons, and prayers; the children's songs and campfire devotions. Imagine if we could take away the baptismal vows taken by her parents, the commitment she made at her confirmation, the covenant she embraced at her wedding, the renewal she experienced with the sacrament. Imagine if we could take away all the daily morning prayers she offered, the blessings before meals, the prayers she taught at the bedside of her children, the intercessions others offered for her. After extracting all these experiences from her life, who would she be?

We would not recognize her as the same person. The lifelong practice of loving God fundamentally changed her. Worship changed how she viewed herself and her relationship with God; it formed her sense of purpose and drew her toward others; through worship, God called

her to make a difference in the world and she responded. In worship, she made the most critical decisions and commitments of her life. Worship gave her depth and coherence, a purpose that was irreplaceable, and that was only achievable by the path she took in following Christ. Her life was saturated with grace. Through worship, she became someone she otherwise never would have become.

The book began with Linda feeling awkward and yet curious about worship. New to worship, she has yet to discover the rhythm, strength, and belonging that comes with the practice of loving God. We end with Helen, for whom worship was life. At whatever stage of faith we find ourselves, God uses worship to reach us, to change our hearts, and to make us God's own. Through worship, we reach for God in return, devoting ourselves with passion so that we begin to see the world through God's eyes. God loves us, and God uses our practice of loving God in return to form us into followers of Jesus Christ.

"I am the vine," Jesus said, "you are the branches" (John 15:5). Worship connects the branches to the vine, keeps us connected to the source of life, and helps us grow in Christ.

Through Radical Hospitality, we invite God into our lives and receive God's gracious love for us. Through Passionate Worship, we love God in return. God uses worship to change our hearts and minds. This creates in us a desire to grow in grace all the more, and this leads us to the next practice of fruitful living, Intentional Faith Development.

REFLECTION

How LOVELY *is your dwelling place,*
O Lord *of hosts!*
My SOUL LONGS,
INDEED IT FAINTS
for the courts of the Lord;
my HEART *and my* FLESH
SING FOR JOY
to the LIVING GOD.

—*Psalm 84:1-2*

"I am the vine," Jesus said, "you are the branches". Worship connects the branches to the vine, keeps us connected to the source of life, and helps us grow in Christ.

Questions

- How has God shaped you through your worship and prayer?

- How have you made worship a priority in your life? What changes would it take to make worship a higher priority?

- How does your love for God strengthen you?

- How can you imagine feeding and fostering your love for God by changing your patterns of prayer and worship?

Prayer

By your Spirit, make us one with Christ, one with each other, and one in ministry to all the world.

Leader Helps
for Small Group Sessions

Loving God in Return

SESSION 1: *Returning God's Love Changes Us*
Focus Point
Worship expresses our love for God and connects us to God.

GETTING READY *(Prior to the Session)*
Preparation
• Read Chapter 1 in Loving God in Return
• Write the key Scripture and focus points on a board or chart.
• Review Digging In and Making Application, and select the points and discussion questions you will cover.
• Acquire a box of index cards and a bag of pens.
• Pray for the session and for your group members.

Key Scripture: *"How lovely is your dwelling place, O Lord of hosts! My soul longs, indeed it faints for the courts of the Lord; My heart and my flesh sing for joy to the living God." Psalm 84*

Main Ideas:
• Worship expresses our love for God in response to God's love for us.
• Worship involves voluntarily setting time aside to focus on God's will rather than our own agenda, to receive God's word rather than merely giving our point of view.
• Worship provides the most likely setting for the change of heart and mind we describe as justification, the moment of conscious awareness and decision that involves our receiving God's grace through Christ, confessing our need for God, accepting God's pardon, and turning our lives toward God and away from former ways.

GETTING STARTED
Opening Prayer
Loving God, we are so thankful for your unconditional and unending love for us. Your love is so amazing that we want to respond by loving and adoring you in return. We long to draw close to you and connect with you in worship, and we know that when we do, we are changed. Help us to make worship a priority in our lives, and teach us to be passionate worshipers. In Jesus' name we pray. Amen.

DIGGING IN *(25–30 minutes)*
FOCUS POINT: Share the Focus Point with the group.

• Review Linda's story from Chapter 1.
• Then, read aloud the paragraph starting, "As the service ended..." (p. 20).

Group Discussion
• Have you ever been the visitor in the worship service? What was your reaction to the various elements of worship?
• When has an invitation felt like a "thread of grace had been cast across a great chasm" for you?
• When have you most recently felt a connection to God in worship?

In the book, Robert Schnase writes that God uses worship to crack open closed hearts and that God reshapes the human soul through worship.

Group Discussion
• When have you felt reshaped by a time of worship?
• Would you say this is the norm or the exception for you? Why?

MAKING APPLICATION

What Does It Look Like?
• Ask a volunteer to read aloud Psalm 84: 1-2.

Briefly discuss
• When was the last time you longed for a time of worship?
• What keeps us from the longing the psalmist describes?

Hand out note cards and pens to each participant. Ask them to write the following questions along with their answers on their note cards. These answers will not be shared, but encourage them to keep this card in their Bibles or books and bring them each week as they will add to the list.

What is your response to God's love for you?
What do you need to change or adjust concerning your feelings about worship?

What Now?
• Ask participants to reflect silently in response to this question:
• In light of all we have shared today, what do you sense God saying to you?

End by inviting answers to these questions:
• In response, what will you do differently this week?
• How will what you learned this week change how you live your life?

Close your session with prayer requests and invite a participant to close in prayer.

Loving God in Return

Focus Point: Worship connects us to God and to others who love God.

GETTING READY *(Prior to the Session)*

Preparation:
- Read Chapter 2 in Loving God in Return
- Write the key Scripture and focus points on a board or chart.
- Review Digging In and Making Application, and select the points and discussion questions you will cover.
- Pray for the session and for your group members.

Key Scripture: *Make a joyful noise to the Lord, all the earth. / Worship the Lord with gladness; / come into his presence with singing. Psalm 100:1-2*

Main Ideas:
- God desires a relationship with us, and in response to God's seeking us, worship is our way of seeking God, our reaching upward to God's reaching downward.
- Worship fosters our relationship to the spiritual aspects of life.
- Worship provides a way by which we let ourselves be found, a way to find God, and to find ourselves.

GETTING STARTED

Opening Prayer:
Loving God, you are so worthy of our praise and worship. You are good and mighty and holy and wonderful. Thank you for the great mystery of faith that you, the Creator of the universe, want to come close to us. We come to you with gladness. Help us to make worship a priority in our lives, and teach us to be passionate worshipers. In Jesus' name we pray. Amen.

DIGGING IN

Emphasize God's activity in worship by reading aloud the following sentences: "The purpose of worship does not begin and end with what human beings do; worship is the means God uses to accomplish God's purposes in the human heart and in the community of Christ. God is active in worship even when we are not."

Group Discussion
• How do these ideas enlighten your understanding or view of worship?
• Why is it important to view worship from God's point of view, and how can this benefit worshipers?

Refer to the heading Without a Sound from Chapter 2 (p. 43).
Group Discussion
• Reflect on your congregation. What are the answers to these questions?

MAKING APPLICATION

What Does It Look Like?

Wrap up the session by reading aloud the passage from Chapter 2 that begins, "The path to fruitful living, to discovering the riches of the spiritual life…" (p. 42).

Ask participants to pull out their note cards from last week. Ask them to write two new questions along with their answers on their note cards. These answers will not be shared, but encourage them to keep this card in their Bibles or books and bring them each week as they will add to the list.
• How often would you say your worship is anything less than passionate? How can you regain a passion for worshiping God?
• What are some ways you reach up to God in worship? How does God reach downward to you?

What Now?
Instruct participants to reflect silently in response to this question:
• In light of all we have shared today, what do you sense God saying to you?

End by inviting answers to these questions:
• In response, what will you do differently this week?
• How will what you learned this week change how you live your life?

Close your session with prayer requests and invite a participant to close in prayer.

Loving God in Return

SESSION 3: *The Mystery of Worship*
Focus Point: There is great mystery in worship.

GETTING READY *(Prior to the Session)*

Preparation:
• Read Chapter 3 in Loving God in Return
• Write the key Scripture and focus point on a board or chart.
• Review Digging In and Making Application, and select the points and discussion questions you will cover.
• Pray for the session and for your group members.

Key Scripture: *The Master, Jesus, on the night of his betrayal, took bread. Having given thanks, he broke it and said, This is my body, broken for you. Do this to remember me. I Corinthians 11:23-24* The Message

Main Ideas:
• There is great mystery in worship.
• Daily personal prayer and worship deepen our relationship with God and prepare us for community worship.
• Passionate worship requires us to surrender or relinquish ourselves and our will—including all external and internal resistances to worship.

GETTING STARTED

Opening Prayer
Loving God, we are in awe of your mystery. You make ordinary things holy. You make broken things whole. You make beauty from ashes. You change our hearts as we learn to worship you more fully. Change us even now, Lord. In Jesus' name we pray. Amen.

DIGGING IN

Read aloud the paragraph from Chapter 3 beginning, "Truth, love, and creativity always come from places we never fully comprehend" (p. 52).
Group Discussion
• What aspects of worship express a sense of mystery?
• Which of these is most significant to you personally? Why?

Refer participants to the heading A Converting Sacrament in Chapter 3 (p. 53). Share the story of Carl's Communion experience together.

Group Discussion
• How did Carl experience the sacrament of Holy Communion as a means of grace? How did it change him and, ultimately, his life?
• Think of an experience of Holy Communion that particularly moved you. What made it especially meaningful?

Acknowledge that music is another element of worship involving great mystery. Somehow it shapes the human spirit.

Group Discussion
• Why do you think music affects us so profoundly?
• Share a time when you felt your spirit moved or lifted up to God by music in worship.
• How does singing make a difference in your spiritual life?

MAKING APPLICATION

What Does It Look Like?
Read the following excerpt from Chapter 3, "We can't develop a meaningful relationship with someone if we don't spend time with them."

Briefly discuss:
• How has this been true in your personal relationships? Your relationship with God?

Hand out pens to each participant. If anyone was gone the previous weeks, give them a blank note card. Tell participants to pull out their note cards from last week. Ask them to write two new questions along with their answers on their note cards. These answers will not be shared, but encourage them to keep this card in their Bibles or books and bring them each week as they will add to the list.
• What resistances do you need to overcome in order to become a passionate worshiper?
• What do you need to do to open yourself more fully to the mystery of grace in worship?

What Now?
Instruct participants to reflect silently in response to this question:
• In light of all we have shared today, what do you sense God saying to you?

End by inviting answers to these questions:
• In response, what will you do differently this week?
• How will what you learned this week change how you live your life?

Close your session with prayer requests and invite a participant to close in prayer.

SESSION 4: *The Practice of Passionate Worship—Renewing Our Love for God.*
Focus Point: Passionate Worship is a dynamic, vibrant expression of a fruitful relationship
with God.

GETTING READY *(Prior to the Session)*

Preparation:
• Read Chapter 4 in Loving God in Return
• Write the key Scripture and focus points on a board or chart.
• Review Digging In and Making Application, and select the points and discussion
questions you will cover.
• Pray for the session and for your group members.

Key Scripture: *But what happens when we live God's way? He brings gifts into our lives,
much the same way that fruit appears in an orchard—things like affection for others,
exuberance about life, serenity. Galatians 5:22-23a* The Message

Main Ideas:
• The practice of Passionate Worship becomes a valued and sustaining pattern that affects
every aspect of one's life.
• Passionate Worship is a dynamic, vibrant expression of a fruitful relationship with God.
• Through Radical Hospitality, we invite God into our lives and receive God's gracious love
for us. Through Passionate Worship, we love God in return. God uses worship to change
our hearts and minds.

GETTING STARTED

Opening Prayer
*Loving God, you are passionate in your love for us. Forgive us for begin less than passionate
about our worship of you. Restore and renew in us a passion to worship you with all we are.
Help us to make worship a priority in our lives, and teach us to be passionate worshipers.
In Jesus' name we pray. Amen.*

DIGGING IN

Highlight some of the characteristics of people who practice Passionate Worship from
the chapter.
Group Discussion
• How do these things contribute to passionate worship? Are they all required for truly
passionate worship? Why or why not?
• Which of these comes most easily to you and why? Which is most challenging and why?

The Practice of Passionate Worship

Ask a volunteer to read Galatians 5:22-23 from their own Bible. Then, re-read the passage from *The Message*.

Group Discussion
• When has affection for others, exuberance, or serenity felt like a gift from God?
• How do these things come about as a result of passionate worship?

MAKING APPLICATION

What Does It Look Like?
Remind participants of Helen's story from Chapter 4 (p. 73). Be prepared to summarize the story, noting the highlights.

Briefly discuss:
• How did Helen's lifelong practice of loving and worshiping God impact her life and the lives of others?
• How does Helen's story encourage you to pursue the practice of Passionate Worship?

What Now?
Instruct participants to reflect silently in response to this question:
• In light of all we have shared today, what do you sense God saying to you?

End by inviting answers to these questions:
• In response to these sessions on Passionate Worship, what will you do differently this week?
• How will what you learned this week and in the book *Loving God in Return: The Practice of Passionate Worship* change how you live your life?

Close your session with prayer requests and invite a participant to close in prayer.

Loving God in Return
The Practice of
Passionate Worship

"You shall love the Lord your God with all your heart, and with all your soul, and with all your strength, and with all your mind; and your neighbor as yourself." —Luke 10:27

_____

_____

_____

_____

_____

_____

_____

_____

_____

_____

Loving God in Return
The Practice of
Passionate Worship

"You shall love the Lord your God with all your heart, and with all your soul, and with all your strength, and with all your mind; and your neighbor as yourself." —Luke 10:27

_____

_____

_____

_____

_____

_____

_____

_____

_____

_____

Loving God in Return
The Practice of
Passionate Worship

"You shall love the Lord your God with all your heart, and with all your soul, and with all your strength, and with all your mind; and your neighbor as yourself." —Luke 10:27

_____

_____

_____

_____

_____

_____

_____

_____

_____

_____

_____

Loving God in Return
The Practice of
Passionate Worship

"You shall love the Lord your God with all your heart, and with all your soul, and with all your strength, and with all your mind; and your neighbor as yourself." —Luke 10:27